# MS. CARRIE'S LITTLE YELLOW BUTTERFLIES

BY

CARRIE BELL HARRELL-WINNS

**Gotham Books**

30 N Gould St.
Ste. 20820, Sheridan, WY 82801
https://gothambooksinc.com/

Phone: 1 (307) 464-7800

© 2023 *Carrie Bell Harrel-Winns.* All rights reserved.

No part of this book may be reproduced, stored in a retrieval system, or transmitted by any means without the written permission of the author.

Published by Gotham Books (December 9, 2023)

ISBN: 979-8-88775-615-8 (H)
ISBN: 979-8-88775-613-4 (P)
ISBN: 979-8-88775-614-1 (E)

Because of the dynamic nature of the Internet, any web addresses or links contained in this book may have changed since publication and may no longer be valid.

The views expressed in this work are solely those of the author and do not necessarily reflect the views of the publisher, and the publisher hereby disclaims any responsibility for them.

"Ms. Carrie's Little Yellow Butterflies"
is dedicated to:
Quell King Turner

In Loving Memory of:
The Late Rev. Thomas S.
&
Sis. Florine Canteen Lance

Mr. Major J. Miller
"Uncle D"

One Yellow Butterfly sat alone on the fence.
It flew away, when it returned, there were two Yellow Butterflies sitting on the fence.

Two Yellow Butterflies sitting on the fence.
The second Butterfly flew away, when it returned, then there were three Yellow Butterflies sitting on the fence.

The second Yellow Butterfly flew away, when it returned, then there were three Yellow Butterflies sitting on the fence.

The third Yellow Butterfly flew away, and when it returned,
then there were four Yellow Butterflies sitting on the fence.

The fourth Yellow Butterfly flew away, and when it returned, there were five Yellow Butterflies sitting on the fence.

The fifth Yellow Butterfly flew away, and when it returned, there were six Yellow Butterflies sitting on the fence.

The sixth Yellow Butterfly flew away, and when it returned, there were seven Yellow Butterflies sitting on the fence.

7

The seventh Yellow Butterfly flew away, and when it returned, then there were eight Yellow Butterflies sitting on the fence.

The eighth Yellow Butterfly flew away, and when it returned, there were nine Yellow Butterflies sitting on the fence.

The ninth's Yellow Butterfly flew away, and when it returned, there were ten Yellow Butterflies sitting on the fence.

10

Lets start again, Lets count the Little Yellow Butterflies from 1 - 10 AGAIN

One Yellow Butterfly sat alone on the fence.
It flew away, when it returned, there were two Yellow Butterflies sitting on the fence.

Two Yellow Butterflies sitting on the fence.
The second Butterfly flew away, when it returned, then there were three Yellow Butterflies sitting on the fence.

The second Yellow Butterfly flew
away, when it returned,
then there were three Yellow
Butterflies sitting on the fence.

The third Yellow Butterfly flew away, and when it returned,
then there were four Yellow Butterflies sitting on the fence.

The fourth Yellow Butterfly flew away, and when it returned, there were five Yellow Butterflies sitting on the fence.

The fifth Yellow Butterfly flew away, and when it returned, there were six Yellow Butterflies sitting on the fence.

6

The sixth Yellow Butterfly flew away, and when it returned, there were seven Yellow Butterflies sitting on the fence.

The seventh Yellow Butterfly flew away, and when it returned, then there were eight Yellow Butterflies sitting on the fence.

The eighth Yellow Butterfly flew away, and when it returned, there were nine Yellow Butterflies sitting on the fence.

The ninth's Yellow Butterfly flew away, and when it returned, there were ten Yellow Butterflies sitting on the fence.

**10**

www.ingramcontent.com/pod-product-compliance
Lightning Source LLC
LaVergne TN
LVHW071700060526
838201LV00037B/396